Chamber Music

by H. Voxman

for THREE SAXOPHONES

CONTENTS...

Rubank®

HAL•LEONARD®
CORPORATION
7777 W. BLUEMOUND RD. P.O. BOX 13819 MILWAUKEE, WI 53213

Be Joyful, Ye Christians

Saxophone Trio

BACH

German Dance

Saxophone Trio

von WEBER

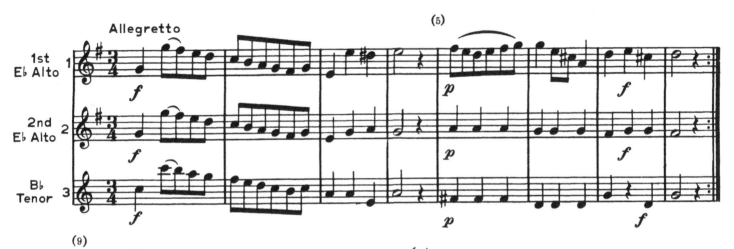

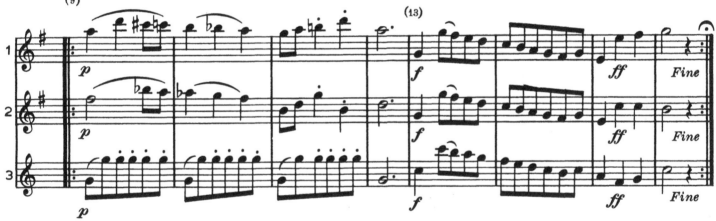

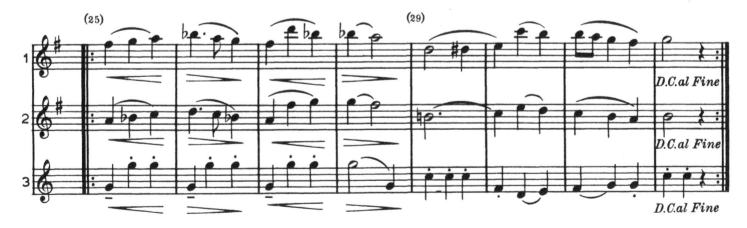

Marche Classique

Saxophone Trio

Eighteenth Century

4

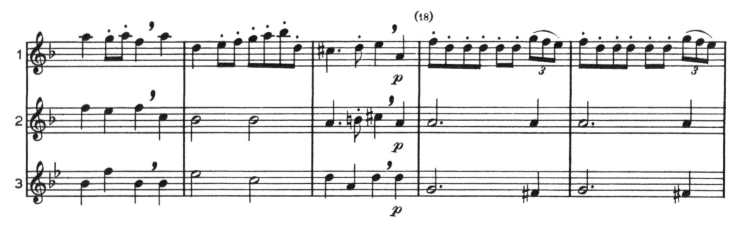

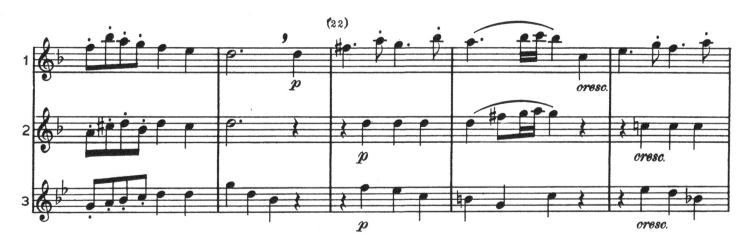

Overture
from Partita in F

Saxophone Trio

FABER

Andante sostenuto

Allegro moderato

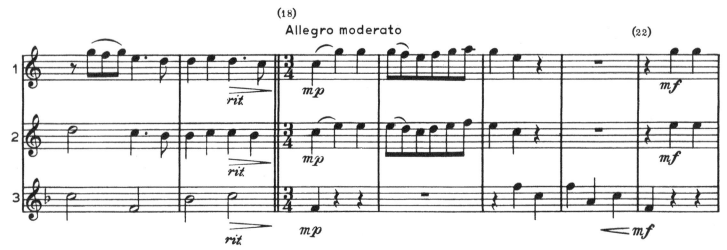

Folk Song Fantasy

Saxophone Trio

American
Arr. by R. Hervig

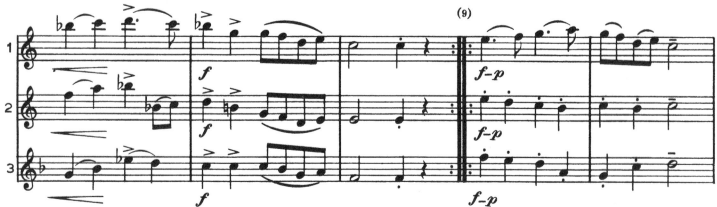

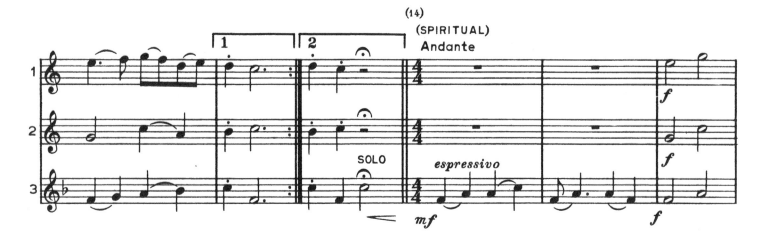

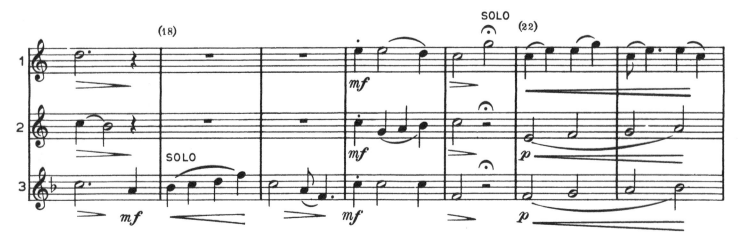

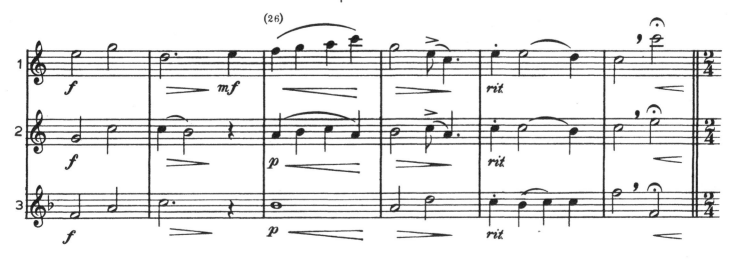

(CHANTEY)
(30) Briskly

Scherzino

Saxophone Trio

HAYDN

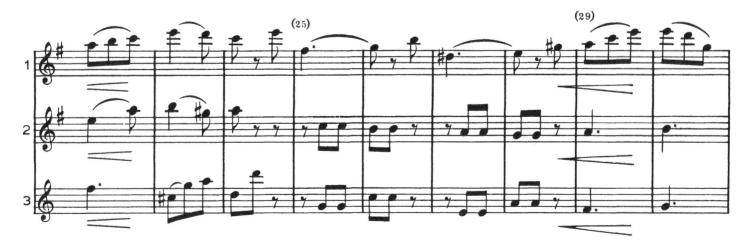

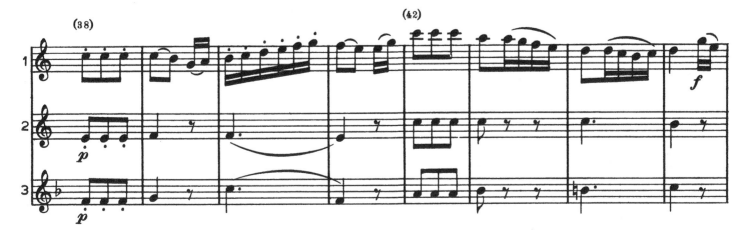

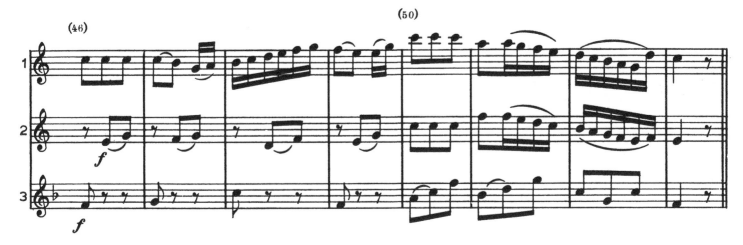

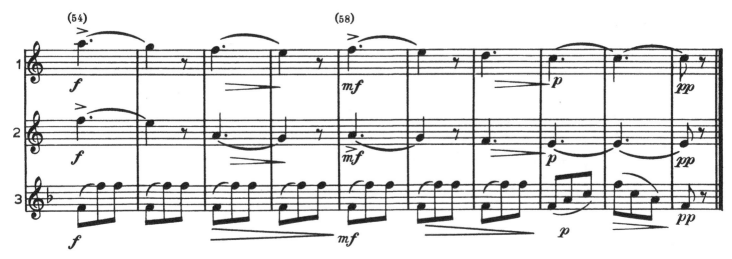

Menuet

Saxophone Trio

SCHUBERT

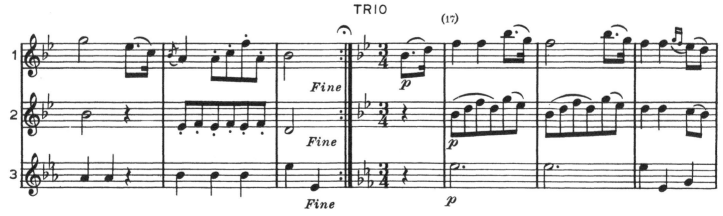

Saxophone Trio

The Monks' Song

BEETHOVEN

Harvest Song

Saxophone Trio

SCHUMANN
Op.68, No. 24

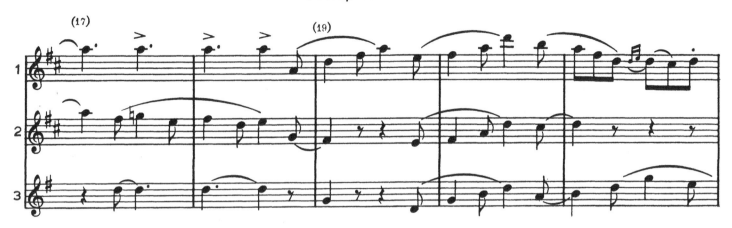

Two Ländler

SCHUBERT

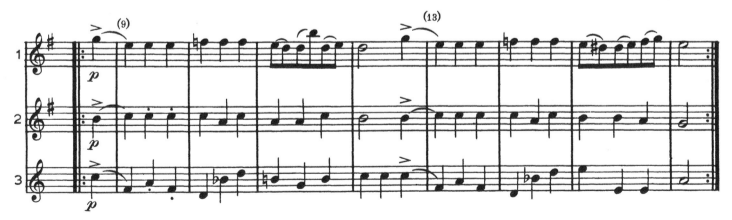

The ländler is an Austrian dance, a kind of slow waltz

Saxophone Trio

Finale
from Trio in G Major

Saxophone Trio

HAYDN

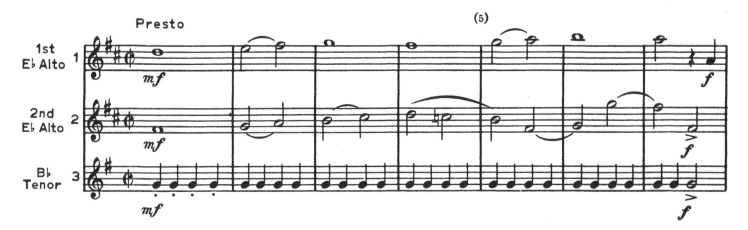

Saxophone Trio

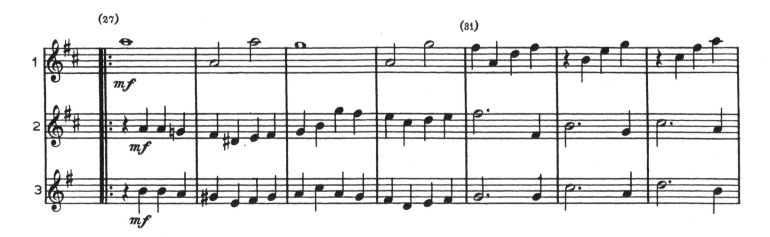

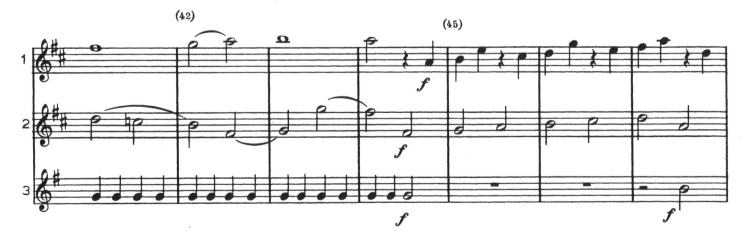

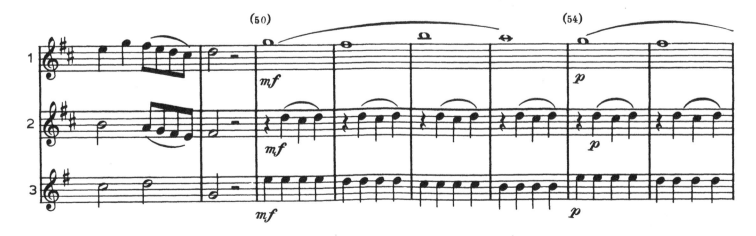

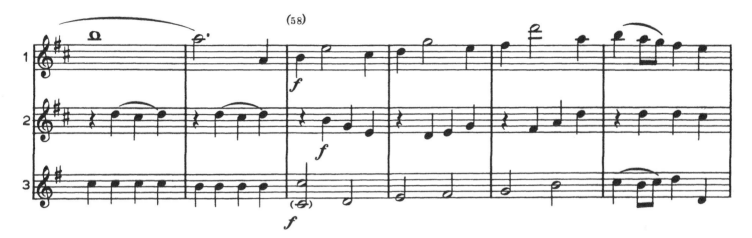

Little Folk Tale

Alsatian

Allegro

from Divertimento II

Saxophone Trio

MOZART

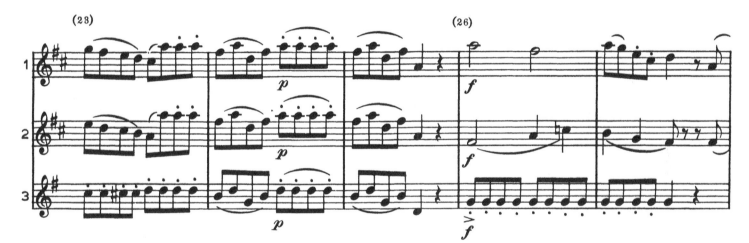

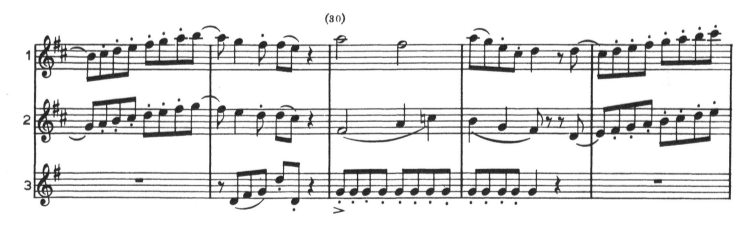

Menuet

Saxophone Trio

MOZART

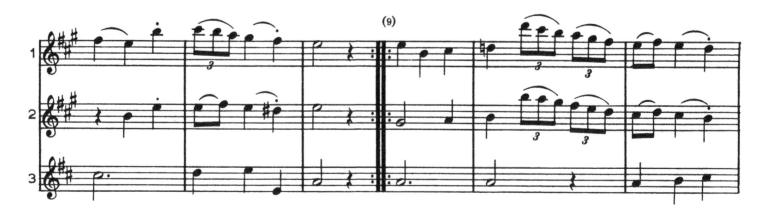

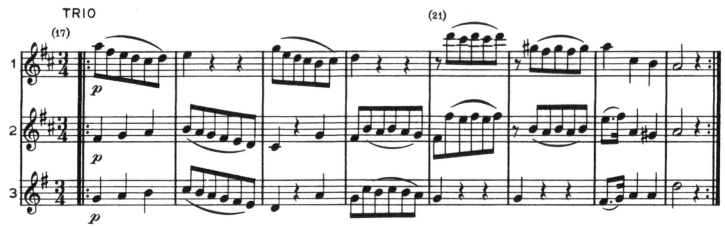

Dolce

TELEMANN

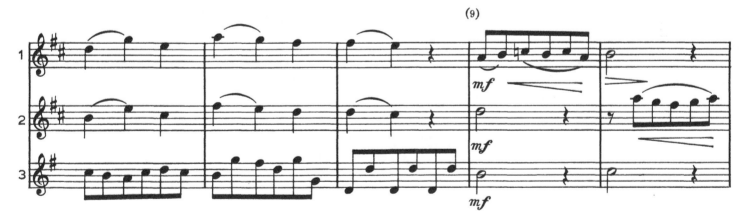

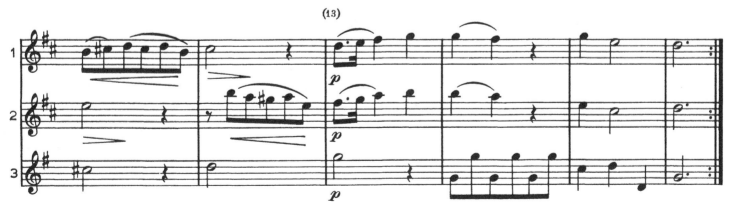

Adagietto
from Sonata, Op.4

Saxophone Trio

BELLA

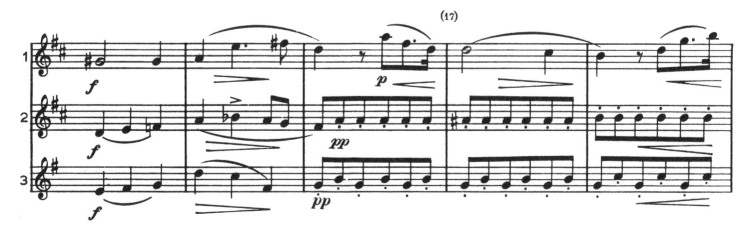

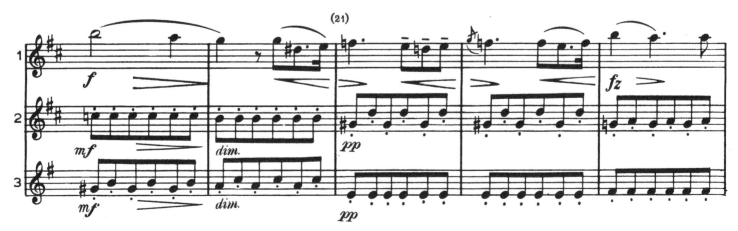

Passepied

Saxophone Trio

DESTOUCHES

Christmas Serenade

Saxophone Trio

Arr. by R. Hervig

(HARK! THE HERALD ANGELS SING)
Moderato

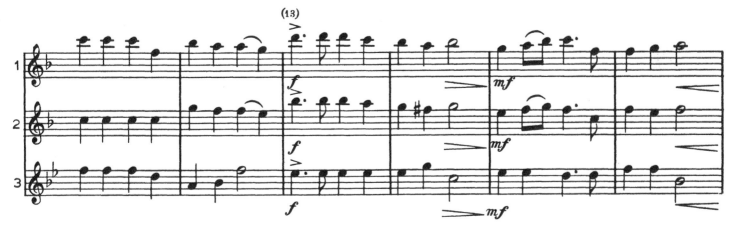

Saxophone Trio

(WE THREE KINGS OF ORIENT ARE)

(JINGLE BELLS)

Saxophone Trio

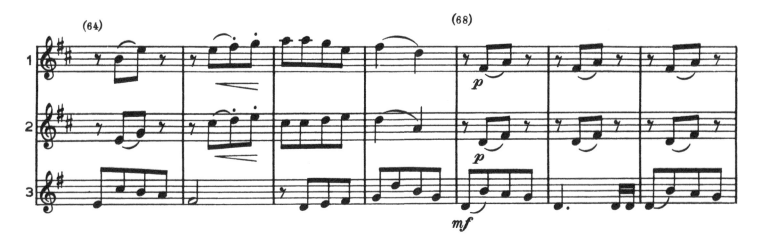

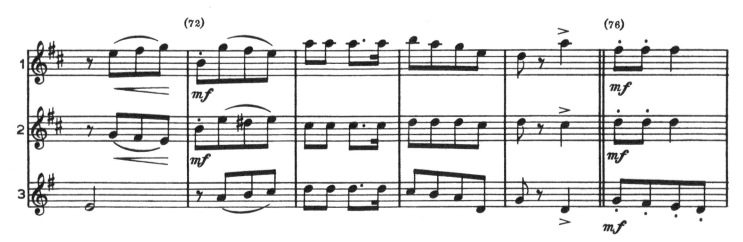

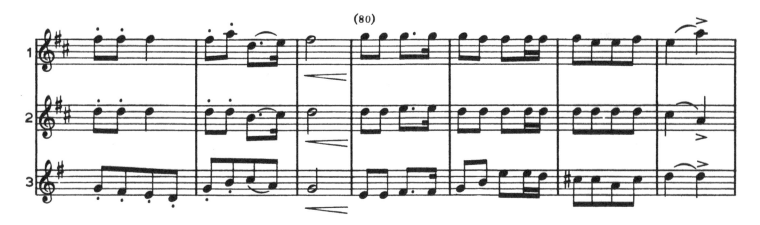

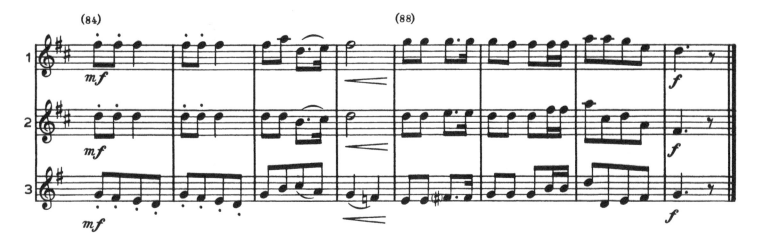

Andante
from Sonata, Op. 83, No. 4

Saxophone Trio

HOOK

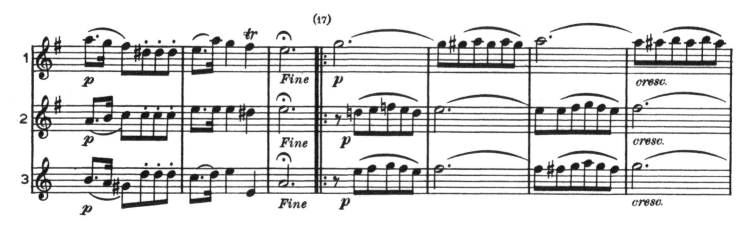

Saxophone Trio

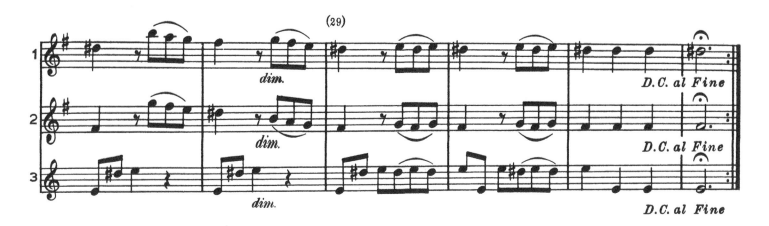

The Mountains Are Steep

BRAHMS
Op. 44, No. 8

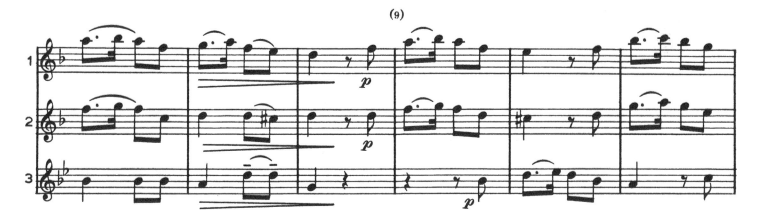

The Miller's Maid

Saxophone Trio

BRAHMS
Op. 44, No. 5